The Tao of Motherhood

The Tao of Motherhood

20th Anniversary Edition

The Tao of Motherhood

Vimala McClure

Illustrations by Tracy Cunningham

New World Library
Novato, California

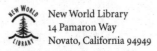 New World Library
14 Pamaron Way
Novato, California 94949

Copyright © 1991, 1994, 1997 by Vimala McClure

Cover and interior design by Tracy Cunningham
Interior illustrations by Tracy Cunningham

Library of Congress Cataloging-in-Publication Data
McClure, Vimala Schneider, date.
The Tao of motherhood / Vimala McClure.—20th anniversary ed.
   p. cm.
Adaptation of: Dao de jing.
Includes bibliographical references (p. 145).
ISBN 978-1-60868-013-9 (pbk. : alk. paper)
1. Motherhood—Religious aspects—Taoism. I. Laozi. Dao de jing. II. Title.
BL1923.M38 2011
649'.1—dc22   2011000438

First printing of twentieth anniversary edition, April 2011
ISBN 978-1-60868-013-9
Printed in Canada on 100% postconsumer-waste recycled paper

 New World Library is a proud member of the Green Press Initiative

10 9 8 7

Dedicated to my mother

Contents

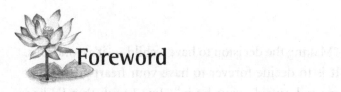
Foreword

Motherhood is both heart-lifting and heart-wrenching. What lifts our hearts more than the sweet experience of having a sleepy baby snuggle cozily into our necks, contentedly making those magical baby sounds? What causes our hearts to soar higher than receiving a spontaneous "I love you, Mom!" accompanied by an enthusiastic hug? What fills us with more quiet joy than watching our children grow into self-confident, happy, and loving adults? For me, family and motherhood have brought the most profound joy and fulfillment of my life.

Paradoxically, along with the joys come the sorrows. And, while my life has been filled to the brim with both bliss and sadness, nothing has caused more excruciating pain than watching my children suffer through illness and trauma, or fearing for their safety, or going through periods of emotional distance from them. Elizabeth Stone described the depth of feeling involved in mothering beautifully when she said,

"Making the decision to have a child — it's wondrous. It is to decide forever to have your heart go walking around outside your body." How I wish that I'd had *The Tao of Motherhood* as a comfort and guide when my four "outside hearts" were little. How thankful I am to have discovered it even now when they are adults! Reading it has helped honor my motherhood and mothering — both the strengths and weaknesses — and helped me relax into the flow of the new adventure of grandparenting. The wisdom of the teachings still apply, for, as we all know, once a mother, forever a mother.

Over the years, I've come to believe that the act of parenting is a cleansing tempest in which our souls are given myriad opportunities to gain new strength, wisdom, and serenity. *The Tao of Motherhood* is a discerning guide, a comforting companion, and a soul friend for those of us navigating the mysterious waters of motherhood. In savoring this book, let it teach you to trust your intuition and to be gentle with yourself as you mother both your own inner child and the children given to your care. I know in my heart that you will find treasures for your soul in Vimala's

shared wisdom and in the inspiration of the remark-
able Taoist teacher Lao Tzu.

— Sue Patton Thoele

Sue Patton Thoele is the author of *Heart Centered Marriage, The
Courage to Be Yourself, The Woman's Book of Courage, The Woman's
Book of Confidence, The Woman's Book of Spirit,* and *Autumn of
the Spring Chicken.*

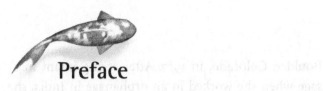

Preface

Many years ago, on a summer's evening, I slipped into a chair on a big porch in Denver, Colorado, and listened to Vimala sing. I sat behind her, hoping that my presence would not disturb the sweet music and devotional sentiment that brought tears to my eyes. Today as I read *The Tao of Motherhood* new tears come and remind me of those tears years ago.

During the first years I knew Vimala in Denver, we both worked in a large house filled with young people trying to guide a spiritual and social service organization. I remember Vimala as a quiet but powerful soul who seemed to stay out of the battles but always got what she needed, someone who sat back and watched what went on and then made the precise move needed to reestablish balance.

When Vimala does take action, she blazes new trails, leaving a clear path behind her for those who might follow. When she had to give birth by caesarean section and felt unprepared for the experience, she helped form the Caesarean Birth Education Group in

Boulder, Colorado, in 1977. After seeing infant massage when she worked in an orphanage in India, she tried it out, very successfully, with her colicky son. She began teaching other parents, and by the time her second baby was born, she was teaching others to be instructors. From those small beginnings has grown the International Association of Infant Massage, which now has over twenty-eight chapters teaching parents in countries around the world, from Europe to Africa and Asia.

When Vimala sees a need, she looks for practical ways in which she can make a difference. When her spiritual teacher was being mistreated in prison, she compiled the evidence and wrote a book to spread the information. When she wanted to learn Bengali, she put together a super learning program to help others and became a proficient speaker in the process. When she fell in love with Bangladesh, she wrote a book for children, called *Bangladesh: Rivers in a Crowded Land*. To help women apply spirituality to their lives, she produced *A Woman's Guide to Tantra Yoga*. While others may talk or complain, Vimala takes action.

First published in 1991, *The Tao of Motherhood* grew out of a period in Vimala's life when she saw her children grow both closer to her and farther away. She watched them become teenagers, struggle with family changes, and make decisions that stretched her as their mother. She formed a new family from two, watching the years it took for balance to settle in.

As with all true artists, both pain and joy have contributed to her work. Vimala has struggled with poverty, health problems, and abuse at different times in her life. But she has taken them and mixed them with deep thought, love, and spiritual bliss and come up with the inspiration and discipline to manifest practical works — works such as *The Tao of Motherhood,* which, though based on an ancient text, helps us parent in a very modern, very stressful world.

One last story to share: I attended a training of infant massage instructors that Vimala was leading in 1984. One father in the demonstration class was particularly rough with his baby, simply because he was a big and tough, but loving, person. When a concerned trainee asked if we shouldn't be trying to temper his enthusiasm in order to protect the baby, Vimala pointed out, "Remember that every child and every parent has a completely unique and special relationship. That child knows his dad and loves his dad. Our job is to watch that communication, to nurture it, and to support the parents in their heart-to-heart relationships with their children." That very practical, yet insightful, philosophy is expressed throughout *The Tao of Motherhood.*

You and your child have a unique and very special relationship. The dos and don'ts of all the advice givers out there may or may not apply to you. You have to listen to your heart and to your child and then make the decisions that are good for right now, for you two.

A lot of water has flowed under the bridge in the thirty-five years I have known Vimala. Both of our children have grown up and gone on to become the people they want to be. But like other mothers and women everywhere throughout time, we still reach out to each other to share our joys and fears, our spirituality, our reality, and yes, our tears.

May your parenting be fulfilling and satisfying for both you and your little ones.

— Jody Wright

Jody Wright is the mother of five grown daughters and lives in Northampton, MA. She was the president of Motherwear, a catalog and website for breastfeeding mothers, for twenty years. She travels extensively as an international instructor and trainer for Infant Massage USA and the International Association of Infant Massage. She is a certified lactation counselor, a La Leche League leader, and an Acharya and meditation teacher for Ananda Marga.

# Introduction

Since before the birth of my first child, parenting has been an important and integral part of my spiritual path. Having meditated daily for several years before my first pregnancy, I wanted to continue my practice. But I knew that pregnancy and young children added a level of chaos into life that seemed to be in conflict with the stillness and quiet — the solitude — of meditation. My search for a way to continue functioning as a spiritual seeker led to much thinking about spirituality and its place in everyday life.

When my first child was born it was time for me to begin practicing in earnest a lesson that was part of my instruction in meditation. The lesson is called *madhuvidya* in Sanskrit (sweet knowledge), and it is the act of infusing spirituality into every aspect of life. It is the conscious process of perceiving the unity of all things, of trying to understand deep within oneself that everything is sacred. Infant massage was a wonderful tool and became an important part of my relationship with my children. I shared this with other parents in my book *Infant Massage: A Handbook for Loving Parents*.

As my children grew our relationships provided so much growth for me. In order to give them what they needed — respect, acceptance, encouragement, boundaries, assistance, understanding, and above all unconditional love — I had to learn about these things for myself. Everything I had learned about spirituality was tested. Children are mirrors; they will always show you exactly what is going on inside of you. Each phase of their growth is an opportunity to heal your own pain, to go deeper inside yourself and become more truly human.

Parenting is a spiritual path that can bring you great pain and great joy and that can have a tremendous positive impact on your personality and your behavior.

I believe our children, unknowingly and with innocent trickery, teach us the deeper knowledge of how to be a true human being.

My heart has learned its lessons from meditation and mothering. This book has given me a chance to distill some of those lessons through the vehicle of the wonderful Taoist teachings of Lao Tzu.

I hope you find inspiration here, and that your journey with your child is a joyful one that teaches you what you came here to learn.

1

oneness

Tao is the oneness of all things.

You and your child come from
One and journey toward One.
You are essentially the same.

Right mothering springs from
this knowledge: the One in either
responds to the One in both.
The bond is oneness, and cannot
be broken.

When doubt and uncertainty arise,
return to this simple truth.

Be in oneness, and the illusion of separateness dies.

Be still and allow unity to be revealed.

2
detachment

Like the eternal Tao, a wise mother
gives birth but does not possess. She
meets the child's needs yet requires
no gratitude.

Observe how great masters raise
up their dearest disciples. Observe
how nature raises up the plants
and animals.

Great teachers take no credit for
their students' growth, yet they
will go to any length to teach
them what they need to know.

Nature requires no praise,
yet it provides for the needs
of earth's inhabitants.

Mother is the reflective principle,
the balancing agent for the child.
Like a guru, she allows the child to
make mistakes and loves the child
without condition. Like nature,
she allows consequences to unfold
and balance to be restored when
it is lost.

She intervenes only when the right use
of power is required.

3
response

Right mothering meets the child's need.

Focusing on what the child should *not* be draws resistant energy. Pointing out what the child *should* be feeds self-hatred and struggle.

Ask yourself, "What is my child telling me about his needs at this moment?" This is not always easy. One child's needs may be more obvious — or more acceptable — than another's.

Meeting needs and obeying
commands are not the same.
The wise obey the Divine Law
and thus fulfill the need of the
moment through action or
non-action. They are responsive,
not tyrannized.

This has nothing to do with what
society says is proper. It has everything
to do with the Infinite Good as it flows
through the here and now.

Do not reward performance.
Rather, respond to Spirit
expressing the Way. You are a
mirror with which your child
sees — and corrects — himself.

4
perspective

Remember, you and your child
are travelers through infinite time.
How you interact is important
enough to change lifetimes of karma;
yet it is an insignificant drop in the
ocean of relationship through which
you both move.

Keep in mind the endless nature
of being, and your journey will
gain perspective.

5
respect

Raise up your children with
great reverence for the Consciousness
that moves in them. Treat them
with respect, even in their infancy,
for they are not yours.

Reverence and respect are not the
same as worship; children thrive on
benevolent neglect.

The child who feels your respect
during silences is nourished more
than the child who is constantly
fussed and chattered over.

6
feminine

Mother is the feminine principle.
She represents the yin, the anima,
the receptive, the earth.
Though she must at times take
the role of the masculine principle,
it is the feminine which gives
her power and from which
she draws her strength.

She teaches her daughters to
respect their feminine nature.
She teaches her sons to respect
their feminine side and thus
all women.

The truly feminine mother
never cringes or defers.
Her strength is unshakable,
like the earth upon which we
walk but which can topple us
with a single deep breath.

7
selflessness

Everything which endures can only do so because Eternal Consciousness gives it sentience.

A mother who gives herself completely to her infant meets herself in the dark and finds fulfillment.

In the hours between midnight and dawn, she crosses the threshold of self-concern and discovers a Self that has no limits. A wise mother meets this

Presence with humility and steps
through time into selflessness.
Infants know when their mothers have
done this, and they become peaceful.

Who, then, is the doer? Is it the infant
who brings its mother through the veil
of self-concern into limitlessness? Is it
the mother, who chooses to hold
sacred her infant's needs and
surrender herself? Or is it the
One, which weaves them both
through a spiraling path
toward wholeness?

You can sit and meditate while
your baby cries himself to sleep.
Or you can go to him and share
his tears, and find your Self.

8
acceptance

Water benefits us without taking
from us. It cleanses us, nourishes us,
and calms our restlessness.

So is a mother to her child. From the
moment of birth, a child's well-being
is her only concern.

A wise mother cleans and discards
the child's waste without comment.
The child's excrement, its tears, its
rages, are all allowed to be and
discarded without emotion.

A wise mother does not judge her child.

9
power

There is great power in being a
mother. It is easy to think you control
your child and his destiny; that you can
mold him into your ideal; that his
imperfections are yours to correct.

The power of a mother's love
is like gold in a temple.
Used for personal aggrandizement
it brings pain and suffering.
Hoarded, it benefits no one.
Used rightly, with benevolence,
in time of great need, it serves.

When you are about to use
your power in your relationship

with your child, think again.
Is there another way to
accomplish your goal?

Retreat and be still. Contemplate your
choices. When you choose to use your
power, use it justly, with great calm,
and do not waver.

10
clarity

Strive for clarity in your own life.
What motivates your feelings?
We often live out the past over
and over in our relationships.
We sometimes fail to see the real
child, for we have superimposed our
own pain upon our children.

Clear yourself. Find the child within
you, heal her, and set her free. As long
as the child in you weeps and cringes,
your power as a mother will remain
confused.

Polish the mirror of the self and your
child will see herself more clearly.

11

empty spaces

The empty spaces make
wholeness. The emptiness in a
pot makes it valuable; you can
fill it with food or water.

Pay attention to what isn't. Listen
for what your child does not say.
Observe what she does not do.

Similarly, know that your child
uses your empty spaces. What
you do not say resounds. What
you do not do impresses.

12

peace

Life with children is naturally noisy.
Can you find the silence within the
noise? Can you feel the peace
within the turmoil?

If you cannot reflect in the chaos
of the moment, withdraw.
Make time for yourself to turn
inward and digest your life.

Whether you realize it or not,
Mother is the pivot of the family.
Not you, but the eternal Mother
expressing Itself through your choices.

To allow the Mother principle
to work to center your family,
take time for yourself.
Otherwise, the self will be
constantly grasping for its share.
This grasping obscures the Mother
principle from within you and
from your family, and leaves
everyone alone and lost.

13
self-care

It is said, "She who values her body
more than dominion over the empire
can be given custody of the empire."
Taking care of yourself is your right
and your responsibility.

If a mother values herself, her
children value her. She teaches
self-esteem by her example.
Her peaceful demeanor
communicates love to all who
come in contact with her.

Knowing when to sacrifice the self and
when to nurture the self comes with
daily mindfulness. Pay attention

to your body's signals. Observing
your feelings each day, eventually
you will be able to take time for
yourself before it becomes an angry
demand. This enables you to give
of yourself appropriately, without
resentment.

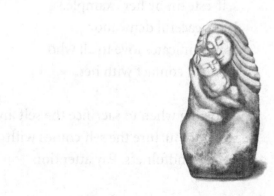

14
love

>⊷⟩⊷⊙⊷⟨⊷⊰

Parenting is at times confusing. There will be moments when you truly do not know. Should you exert your authority or step back? Should you give advice or remain silent? Should you offer help or allow a mistake to be made?

When you cannot see what is happening, relax and look gently with your inner eye. The harder you try to take hold of a situation, the more difficult it becomes.

Let go. Trust in the Way
which follows its own flow.

Allow the Great to live in you
and work through you
for your child's greater good.

Return to the core: a relationship
of love is more worthwhile than
a philosophical position. When
doubt arises, give way only to love.

15
our foremothers

The ancient teachers demonstrated
their realization of the Way.
These ancient teachers were often
women. They were mothers and
sisters, aunts and grandmothers.
They meditated. Through their
relationships, they taught the
art of being.

Because they meditated, their
depth made them seem inscrutable
and their wisdom profound.
The truth is, they simply knew
how to be human.

They observed behaviors and acted with precision and care, never acting recklessly. They behaved with dignity and grace and won the respect of others without trying. They respected others and treated children as human beings.

They were strong yet yielding, like ice ready to melt. They were simple, like the uncarved block of wood. They were receptive, like a valley between high mountains. They were full of life and involved in their families, yet they were able to be still and become as deep and clear as pure water.

These ancient grandmothers did not need to go away into the caves or forests to become enlightened. They were enlightenment itself.

16
awareness

Everything arises from
Consciousness and returns.

The universe is the play of the
rising and returning of millions
of beings, all becoming One.
You and your child are both on
this path too.

It is impossible to keep this
awareness of your destiny
awakened all the time. But daily
meditation can bring awareness
to your thoughts and actions.

Awareness brings constancy to
your relationships. Constancy allows
your child to release fear and follow
his destiny.

Meditate on Oneness. Release the
small self to the Infinite, and the
Infinite will take care of Itself.

17
trust

A wise mother does not unnecessarily interfere with her child's life.

Your children have their own process — their own thoughts, feelings, and reactions — which must be allowed to unfold.

If your childhood was painful, you may get overinvolved with your children's lives and smother them. Or you may find yourself forcing them to think and feel the way you do, to adopt all your values and live the life you wish you had.

If you do not trust your children's process, your children will not trust anyone or anything. Your confidence in them builds their confidence in themselves.

Assist your children in such a way that they think, "We did it ourselves!"

18
hypocrisy

When you forget that you and your children are instruments of the One, dogma takes over.

You begin to think in judgments of yourself and others:

"All mothers should *(stay home, have a career, be involved with school, help with homework, keep a spotless home…)*, therefore I'm not a good mother if I don't."

Or, "All children should *(be polite, respect their elders, help at home,*

get good grades, win in sports, be
popular, appreciate good music, read
great books…), therefore my children
are bad if they don't."

When truth is forgotten, acceptance,
tolerance, compassion, and flexibility
give way to judgment, intolerance,
meanness, and rigidity.
Hypocrisy follows.

Children who are closer to their birth
and thus to the experience of Oneness,
rightly reject hypocrisy.

19
return

>—I—⟨⟩—O—⟨⟩—I—<

Throw away gadgets. Discard
expert opinions. Forget the toys
to stimulate intelligence. Don't buy
devices to simulate what is real.

Return to the real. Connect with
your children heart to heart.
Let them gaze at you, at trees
and water and sky. Let them feel
their pain. Feel it with them.

Touch them with your hands,
your eyes, and your heart.
Let them bond with the living,

breathing world. Let them feel
their feelings and teach them
their names.

Return to the uncarved simplicity.

20
education

<small>━━◆━━◉━━◆━━</small>

The real education teaches us to
be whole human beings.

Be concerned with this: that you,
your marriage, and your home
teach health and balance and truth.

Any further education merely
augments this basic course.

21
spirituality

The wise remain aware of the
spirituality of life.

Every mother has felt the
stillness and the stir of Eternal
Consciousness in her womb.
Remember that.

Bring that mysterious, silent moment
into the clamoring present.

22
surrender

Truth is in paradox:

Surrender and you get
everything. Bend and be strong.

When you reach your limit and
are exhausted, new energy rises
in you. When you release
others, they come to you.
The wise know this: Let go
in order to preserve.

Be empty and fulfilled.

23
stop

There is no natural pouring-forth
that lasts forever. When it rains, it
stops. The wind blows, and then
it ceases.

Learn to use your words wisely,
to communicate rather than to lecture.
Speak your truth, state your feelings,
then stop. Your actions, in silence,
speak louder and will be heard.

Teach your children this:
A human being is greater than
a human doing.

24
security

Your children are not you.

To try to show the world what a good mother you are diminishes you. To try to show the world what good children you have diminishes them.

Heal your insecurity by holding to the truth. The One Consciousness flows through all without boasting.

25
dependence

Eternal Consciousness is not
a thing. It has many names and
no name. It is within and beyond
everything. It is the essence of
us all.

Your child depends on you. You
depend on the earth. The earth
depends on the universe. The
universe depends on the Supreme.

The Supreme is subject to
nothing. It is the Great Mother,
and She holds you in the palm
of her hand.

26
center

Pay attention and stay centered.

You carry the mantle of "Mother,"
the eternal principle of balance and
stability.

When your children's energy is
scattered, be grounded. When
your children throw tantrums,
be still. Know what you stand for.

Be firm and consistent to teach your
children about boundaries. Thus you
will root them in health and release
their souls to limitlessness.

27
knowledge

Someone who travels often knows the best routes. Someone who speaks for a living knows when to pause. Someone who works with numbers knows how to add and subtract in her head.

A wise mother knows: It is her state of consciousness that matters.

Her gentleness and clarity command respect. Her love creates security.

To learn the Way, children need to respect the Mother. To learn the Way, mothers need to cherish the Child.

Thus each follows nature and finds the Self.

28
healing

A mother must know how to assert
her warrior side, how to wield power
and make decisions, how to inspire
discipline and set boundaries. But she
must hold to the feminine to be truly
effective.

The most powerful mothers are
healers. Their surgeon's knives cut
but do not sever. They nourish
and listen.

A wise mother knows the One
Consciousness works through her.

29
intervention

Avoid pushing too hard. Your
children are full of spirit and
will find their way. Their true
parent resides within them;
you are only a reflection.

Mothers who constantly interfere
— who push and challenge,
who lecture and berate —
think they are molding their
children into good citizens.
In fact, they are destroying
confidence and inviting scorn.

Know when to intervene and how.
Do it with gentleness, firmness,
swiftness, and respect. And then
release the child to the Way.

30
conflict

~∗~◇~∗~

Your children will challenge you
and your power. Do not use force
or intimidation to manage them.

Remember, wars bring suffering to all.
The winners and the losers both have
bitter harvests.

When your child engages you in
conflict, bring it full circle without
physical, mental, or emotional
violence.

Withdraw, be still. Try to
understand what the child needs,

whether it be a firm boundary
or a listening heart. Then calmly
exert your authority with love,
end the conflict and restore
harmony.

31
anger

When you feel angry with your
child, know that something
rational must be done. State your
feelings honestly, then withdraw to
process your emotions and make a plan.

Striking out, either physically
or emotionally, may succeed in getting
through to the child, but it will also
plant the seeds of guilt. Guilt is followed
by resentment and bitterness. A victory
can therefore end in failure.

Too many such victories and you will
witness the death of your child's trust.

32
the way

The Way cannot be defined;
it is only when you are in its flow
that it becomes known to you.

If parents, the guardians of the
human race, could hold to the Way,
children would naturally grow strong
and healthy in body, mind, and spirit.
Nothing special would be needed.

Because we have forgotten
the Way, road maps and
instructions have come into being.

One must know when to put aside
the instructions and find the Way.

The single most important
instruction is this: Meditate on
the Eternal. As the river finds
the sea, you will find the Way.

33
contentment

You can know your children with
some intelligence. Knowing
yourself requires enlightenment.

You can manage your children with
strength. Mastering your own life
requires true power.

To accept what you are is to be content,
and contentment is the greatest wealth.
To work with patience is to gather
power. To surrender to the Eternal flow
is to be completely present.

34
the eternal source

Eternal Consciousness is
everywhere, in everything.
Everything depends on it
and it guides all things.

Though it is the source of every
atom of the universe, nothing can
affect it. No one can own it.
It lives in every blade of grass
and every human being, without
discrimination.

A wise mother is like the
Eternal One. She shines in her
children's eyes.

35
values

If you hold to the Eternal
in thought, word, and action,
your children will return
again and again to you.

Your children may not
understand the depth of your
parenting until later. They may
question your values and say
you are "weird" or not like
other kids' parents.

They may say your life is boring or
strange. Never mind. The wise are
not caught up in appearances.

The Way is at times boring in
its simplicity. Hold to it. The
superficial eventually repels.

That which is real attracts every
good thing to it.

36
upside down

If you want to know what to do,
learn to look at things upside down.
To receive, you must give. Those who
boast are insecure. Silence speaks
louder than words. The strongest
warrior never shows his sword.
The soft overcomes the hard.

Here is an exercise: When you
feel a hardness come around
your heart, go soft and explore
the sensations and feelings that
arise. Feel what is beneath anger:
thousands of tiny moments of pain,
confusion, doubt, fear, self-protection.

Accept all this as part of you.
Look on yourself with kindness.

Now notice the quality of your heart.
How different it is from the hard edge
of control that springs from fear.

37
doing

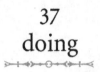

A wise parent does little,
yet so much gets done!

After all, the Eternal does nothing,
yet the entire universe goes on.

When you get too busy, stop and return
to center. When you are centered, you
easily keep things in order. When things
are in order, there is not much to do.

A wise parent does little,
yet so much gets done!

38
choice

If you leave parenting to
the unconscious process, you
will blindly repeat unhealthy
parenting you may have received.

If your childhood was not happy
and secure, you may try too hard
to be an ideal parent.

There are choices to be made every
day. Reject the rigid and favor the
firm. Reject criticism and favor
support. Reject permissiveness and
favor negotiation. Reject abandonment
and favor direction.

Choose the fruit, not the flower.
Choose the berry, not the chaff.
Choose the inner, not the outer.

Conscious choice is the hallmark of
healthy parenting.

39
nature

There is a natural order of things:
the seasons change, the tides well up
and recede, the moon circles and
women's bodies respond.

The sky is clear. The earth is solid.
The unseen forces are powerful.
The valley is full of life. Every atom
dances with Consciousness.

Look around: Everything follows its
nature; wholeness results.

Imagine what would happen if
nature did not follow its biological
programming.

The sky would shatter. The earth would explode. The unseen forces would run amok. The valley would go barren. Everything would lose Consciousness and die into the void.

Oneness is the root of balance. When you can follow your own nature in balance, you will provide exactly what your children need.

40
being

We all come from the One and
return to it.

Stop and bring your consciousness
into this moment. Let your heart
absorb your mind. Can you feel
the oneness that connects you with
your child?

Surrendering to the One is the Way.

Everything comes from Being.
Being springs from that which
is beyond Being.

41
listening

A wise mother learns each day
from quiet listening. Her
parenting springs from her
children's changing needs.

An average mother hears the
lessons but wonders how to be,
and forgets what she learns.
She is often filled with guilt
and is indecisive and irritable.

A foolish mother dismisses
what her soul hears in favor of
what the experts tell her.
She is rigid and controlling,
boastful and full of fear.

The best parenting springs from
simple love. The wise attune
themselves to a child's true need and
steadfastly follow it. Thus, they cannot
be called "permissive" or "harsh."

What is right for each child may not
be right for all children. What is right
cannot always be proven in a laboratory.

42
cycles

The One is born from beyond One. One becomes two, and two becomes three.

That which is beyond consciousness gives birth to consciousness, which gives birth to mind, which gives birth to matter and all the ten thousand things. The ten thousand things maintain a balance between centrifugal and centripetal forces.

The ten thousand things hold Eternal Consciousness within them and thus are magnetized back to the One.

Things harmonize opposites and seek
the One.

You must be a child to be a parent.
The infant is parent to its mother.

To move in balance toward One, make
sure you learn more from your child
than you teach her.

43
softness

Soft overcomes hard.
Who you are means more to
your child than what you teach.

When your heart is hard and
the bitter taste of strong words
is in your mouth, step back.

Let mind go into soft heart.
Breathe kindness and
remain quiet.

44
release

Which is dearer to you:
being right or being respected?

Being respected or being loved?

Having or being?

Know when to let your child go,
to have her own life and feelings.
Your security is within you,
not within your child.

Grasp and you will lose.
Release and find contentment.

45
serenity

The best mothering
looks like no mothering.

Smothering heats up, stillness
cools. Be a still, cool stream
for your child's agitation.

A serene mother rocks
the universe in her arms
and all is well.

46
war

When your life is in order,
your child finds balance.

When you cease to listen with
your heart, war breaks out.
When you lose sight of the big
picture, you fight and quarrel
over trifles and no one wins.

There is no greater pain
than feeling you are not enough.

Your child is enough, right now,
just the way he is. And so are you.

47
what matters

All you need to know
is within you.

Your child's spirit teaches
you how to guide her.

Be present. What is happening
right now? Be still and comprehend
with your inner senses. Talk to the
inner child, setting aside theories.

If your child was taken from
you tomorrow, would this
matter today?

48
relax

First-time mothers read all the books
and cling to theories and gadgets.

Fifth-time mothers have taken it all in
and let it sink into the unconscious.
Equipment has worn out and the child
is given wooden spoons and the easy
company of present-focused people.

The youngest child is usually the most
relaxed!

49
the particular

Be open to your child's individual
needs and expression. One child
needs stimulation, the next needs
quiet. One needs to be carried all
the time, another likes to play
nearby with the freedom to
extend his limbs.

A wise mother knows: There is
no good child and no bad child.
There is only *this* child.

50
fear

When you have your first child,
suddenly life becomes precious.
So precious you can strangle it
with the tension of holding on.

What mother hasn't had fearful
fantasies of losing her child?
This is the hardest time to accept
letting go as part of holding on.

Three mothers in ten grasp their
children with claws of steel
to protect them from harm.

Three mothers in ten allow their
children to wander into danger.

Three mothers in ten confuse their
children with endless admonitions
and worries, yet force them to face
pain before they are ready.

Only ten percent accept the wheel
of life as it is. They are free from fear,
for they know that nothing is ever
lost. They do not grasp and cling or
organize their lives around a
fantasy of what might happen.

For their children, fear cannot find
a place to lodge its blade.

51
flow

Everything comes from One
Consciousness. The harmonious
rhythms we call happiness.
The discordant rhythms
we call pain.

Your child is attracted to the One
in you, to the Way which nurtures,
shelters, guides, and protects. It flows
from you, harmonious with the world
from which your child has come.

The Supreme nurtures
without grasping, shelters without

claiming, guides without
interfering, and protects
without smothering.

The closer you are to the Way,
the more your child will
trust you.

52
significance

The Mother of all is that from
which you draw your mothering.
It is the eternal balance, the
breathing, beating womb from
which all creation arises.
It is eternally giving birth,
eternally conceiving.

Close your mouth and allow
the Mother of all to speak in you.

Keep busy, fluttering and
chattering, and you cannot
hear Her voice.

Observe the child to know
the mother.

Observe the insignificant to know
what matters.

53
consumption

A wise mother keeps her child's life
simple. She gives away ten thousand
toys and keeps only that which is useful.

She lets her baby gaze into her face
and at the wondrous colors of nature.

She gives her child household things
and tells stories the same way over
and over.

Feeling that you must have
every toy, every device, every piece
of equipment merely places objects
between you and your child.

You have to work that much harder
to provide them; work which robs your
child of his most important stimulation
— your company.

Those who become trapped in
the cycle of getting and having spend
their children's lives in a kind of fog.
The best moments are lost forever.

Ask the question: Who really
benefits from all this
consumption?

54
influence

Right mothering is honored from
generation to generation. Like an old
tree with untold roots, it holds firm
through countless storms.

Behave toward yourself with
loving kindness, and serenity
will emanate from you.

When you are serene,
your life is in order.

When your life is in order,
your family is harmonious.

Your family affects your
community. Your community
influences your culture.
Your culture influences the world.

How do I know?
Just by looking around.

55
attunement

The energy that comes from the
Infinite moves through you and
enlightens your being.

When you have released your fear
and found your Self, you can
be in harmony with your child
because you are attuned to
the same energy.

In this space you are relaxed
and soft, bendable. Things don't
bother you, energy flows.

You can walk the baby all night long;
her cries do not challenge you.

Your power is in place
without exerting it.

56
approval

A wise parent knows her intuition
is the only authority worth listening
to. She understands its function and
filters advice through it.

Rigid styles characterize the insecure
parent who needs to protect her
own inner child with fear. She is
full of "don'ts."

A wise parent refrains from
too much talk. Her inner calm
brings peace to troubled hearts and
resolution to conflicts. She doesn't
need anyone's approval but her own.

57
be firm

At each stage of your child's life
she needs demonstrations of
your love and your support.

Your love comforts and accepts.
It is a mirror in which your child
sees herself as beautiful and worthy.

Your support encourages and
affirms; it is a springboard toward
independence.

Too many rules turn facilitation
into interference, affection into
business. Let your child help set

her own limits against which
she can push now and then.

Be firm without being rigid.
Your child will grow up with
lots of healthy personal power.

58
healthy parenting

Healthy parenting can be a challenge if your own childhood wasn't healthy. It requires energy, attention, and constant restraint. These all come naturally from healthy parent-child bonds.

If the parenting you received was rigid, abandoning, or inconsistent, you may find yourself exhausted by your children. Realize that you need healing. Take time out to nurture yourself.

You can make the choice to be a
healthy parent. You can learn how
to trust what is happening and behave
appropriately. You can find a healthy
model and follow it.

Unhealthy parenting disables
with wounds that are hard to heal.
Right mothering is a potent healer,
readily available to the natural
wounds of life.

59
restraint

In bringing up children there
is nothing like restraint. This
requires deep roots in your own
spirituality, because it means
releasing your own ideas in favor
of perceiving each child's needs.

Prayer, meditation, and the like
can help you stay centered
and aware of the deeper levels
of what is happening. Take the
time you need for your
spiritual growth.

Cultivate limitlessness,
and you will know how and
when to set limits for your
children.

60
mirror

As much as possible, let your
children find their own way. Mother
them delicately, like frying eggplant.

Negative states will arise, express,
and pass away. Allow this to happen.
Help the child to become aware of
this process gently, without intrusion.
The wise parent does not fight fire
with fire.

Be a mirror. Let your child see how
cause and effect works in life. Too
much interference and advice gives
power to opposing forces.

61
independence

The mother's energy is so powerful because of her feminine receptivity. She yields and conquers through her calm.

The child's energy dominates. He feels so powerful! Only the mother knows it is her strength upon which he draws to build himself.

Thus both reach their goal of independence.

62
no blame

Knowing how things work
is helpful to you. But remember,
mothers have mothered since the
dawn of time, and it all seems to
work out in the end.

If you don't know your intuition,
it is no crime. However, if you know
how things work, you are fortunate.
Your behavior will be more effective,
your words will have more power,
your decisions will be good ones.

Since ancient times people have
revered those whose spiritual faculties
are well developed.

63
assistance

If you want to help your children
build themselves, you must act without
seeming to act. Through gestures, small
words, and most of all through your
own example, your children will
gradually grow wings.

Your baby is learning to trust you.
Touch and hold her and smile
into her eyes. Allow her to feel
all her feelings.

Your toddler is learning to trust
the earth. Support and protect him.
Allow him to explore.

Your preschooler is learning to trust herself. Help her learn appropriate choices. Allow her to say no and test her limits.

Your young child is learning to trust relationships with others. Affirm his ability to learn how to express his feelings and ask for help. Allow him to ask questions.

Your older child is learning to trust society. Provide accurate information, offer problem-solving tools, and encourage responsibility. Allow her to experience consequences while remaining safe in your love and support.

Your adolescent is learning to
trust himself as an adult.
Celebrate his growing up. Talk
about your own feelings at his
age. Allow him to explore choices
that may be different from yours.

Know your child's needs at each
stage and anticipate her struggles.
In this way you can offer assistance
without seeming to assist.

64
now

Love your children while they
are small. Spend time with them
now. Don't put it off for a
single moment.

The rigid tree begins as a pliant
sapling. A huge building begins
as a shovelful of dirt. A thousand-mile
journey begins under your feet.

Everything depends on early influences.
You can't go back later and bond with
your children in the same way.

Many parents get anxious with their teenagers and try to make up for lost time. When the child needs wings, they try to root him and spoil everything.

Conscious mothering requires careful choices, from beginning to end.

65
experts

The ancient mothers knew. There
was no need for books and experts.

Today we have lost much.
We need to relearn the Way.

Be cautious about what the experts
tell you. What sounds complex
and clever may have no roots.
Wisdom has no cleverness in it.
It is pure and simple, and when it
is practiced the results are obvious.

The wise assist a child's being rather
than his doing.

66
equanimity

The sea is the greatest of all the
waters because it allows the rivers
and streams to empty into it.

Parents with the greatest power in their
children's lives are those to which the
child can go without fear.

The wise mother facilitates her child's
growth with firm, loving kindness.
She receives his mistakes and tantrums
with equanimity.

Because she does not push, harass,
or manipulate, she does not invite

rebellion. Her children love and respect her and trust her with their pain.

67
your treasures

> ⤜◆⟡◆⤛

Everyone says the Eternal One
is great. Because it is great it is
beyond our comprehension.
If we could hold it in our minds,
it would be limited. If it is limited,
it is not the Way.

There are three treasures which
are invaluable to you as a parent:

The first is kindness. The second is
simplicity. The third is humility.

If you are kind, you can act with
courage to support and protect your
children.

If you keep your life simple, you have
lots of time to give them.

If you know yourself as a human being
— no more, no less — you teach your
children without imposing on them.

A parent who is protective without
being kind, whose life is busy and
complicated, who demands respect
and expects perfection, loses her
children in the end.

Loving kindness, simplicity, and
humility are the treasures your
children will inherit.

68
empowerment

A good soldier is never hateful.
A good fighter is not angry.
A good employer encourages
leadership.

The best parenting shows
choices rather than
delivering ultimatums.

Empowerment is the natural
means to grow a good
human being.

69
battles

When your children push against
their limits and your boundaries,
consider the advice of the ancient
strategists: do not allow yourself
to be baited into fighting fire with
fire. Keep your center. Calmly and
clearly show them their choices.

This is winning the battle without
showing your sword.

If you try to overpower your children
you will discover a simple truth:
their power is greater than yours!

Thus you surrender your treasure
and respect is lost.

In a battle of wills, loving kindness
is the only weapon that conquers.

70
a road less traveled

Bringing up children in this way is
easy to understand and easy to do. But
not many parents are able to follow it.

The Way is ancient and follows
truth. It is known to those who are
truly human. But parents today have
lost their roots and rely on the latest
gimmicks and the opinions of
medical technicians.

The wise are known only by a few.
Their wisdom is concealed. The wise
mother's precious gem is hidden in
the pocket of her apron.

71
don't know

Admit you don't know
everything. Admit you may
not know anything.

To pretend that you know
when you don't leads to pain.
When you are tired of pain,
you will no longer create it.
This is the secret of good health.

72
wonder

Children who grow up with no
spirituality — with no sense of wonder
— will struggle with depression as adults.

Do not impose rational thinking
on your children too early. Do not
oppress them with adult reality.

Because you don't pressure them to
grow up, they can grow naturally
and keep their sweetness.

The wise parent can be childlike
but is not irresponsible,
loves herself but is not selfish.
She is spiritual but not dogmatic.

73
courage

There are two kinds of courage.

There is the passionate bravery
which gets people killed.
This kind of courage is inherent;
either you have it or you don't.
It is the bravery of a mother who
would die shielding her child from
a killer's bullet.

The second type of courage is
developed through daily practice.
It is the inner strength to do what
must be done, to make rational plans
and carry them out, to face difficulty
and overcome obstacles.

It is the bravery of a mother
who makes personal sacrifices
for her children's well-being,
and then is able to let them go
to their own destinies.

74
punishment

Many parents discover too late that
one cannot raise children well with
punishment as the core of discipline.
Hit your child and eventually the child's
rage will be greater than your censure.

Prisons are filled with "well-disciplined"
people.

A good parent helps a child to
learn how his behavior affects
his own life through natural
consequences. This is how true
inner discipline is cultivated.

A master carpenter cuts cleanly and quickly and makes furniture which endures. When you deliver harsh, judgmental consequences, you are trying to do nature's job. Like an inexperienced carpenter, you are bound to make a mess of it and only hurt yourself.

75
criticism

Children starve if their parents
eat all the food.

Children rebel if their parents
brook no compromise.

Children have no love for life if
their parents squeeze it out of them.
They spend their lives grieving for
their lost joy.

Begin to notice when you are
critical and controlling with your
child. Observe yourself and check
your behavior before it gets
acted out.

Find out what you need and
give it to yourself. When the little
child in you gets the love, support,
and encouragement it needs,
your critical behavior will
naturally disappear.

76
flexibility

Human bodies are gentle and
flexible when living but hard
and stiff when dead.

Living plants are tender and
green when living but dry and
brittle when dead.

To be hard and unbending is to
be dead. Without flexibility, there
is no juice. What is the point of
living then?

77
balance

When people are in harmony
with spiritual laws, everything is
in balance. The excess is reduced,
the deficient is expanded, everyone's
needs are met, and life is full of joy.

When we lose the Way, we lose our
balance and life is full of pain. We take
from those who do not have enough
and give to those who have too much.

A mother who walks in balance has
more than enough. She enters her
children's lives and surrounds them
with love when their heart-reserves

are low. She allows them to do the
same for her.

She understands the cyclic nature
of things, the way the bow
contracts and expands to receive
and release the arrow.

78
paradox

There is nothing more receptive
and flowing than water,
yet there is nothing better
for polishing stone.

A mother's nature is paradox.
Your strength is in gentleness.
Your authority is in receptivity.
Your power is in letting go.

79
resolution

As your children grow up,
there is bound to be some
unresolved pain. There was the
time you couldn't make it to the
third-grade play. The time you
struck your child in anger. The
painful divorce which could not
be adequately explained.

A wise parent recognizes her
failings and accepts what is.
There is room in life for remorse,
and for forgiveness. There is
room in our hearts for ourselves,
and for one another.

80
simplicity

Keep your life simple,
and serenity will follow.

Like a small country with little
need for supersonic travel,
a simple life has little need for
tension and stress.

Give your children yourself, and
the need for things will be minimal.

81
honesty

Tell the truth.

Say what is happening.

Allow what is, and allow it to be known.

Bring your children up in a home that is clean and clear and honest. There is no greater legacy you can give them.

Bibliography

English, Jane, and Gia-Fu Feng, translators. Lao Tsu. *Tao Te Ching*. New York: Vintage Books, 1972.

Heider, John. *The Tao of Leadership*. Atlanta: Humanics New Age, 1985.

Iyer, Raghavan, Ed. Lao Tzu. *Tao Te Ching: The Book of Perfectibility*. London: Concord Grove Press, 1983.

Lau, D. C., translator. Lao Tzu. *Tao Te Ching*. London: Penguin Books, 1963.

Waley, Arthur. *The Way and Its Power*. New York: Grove Press, 1958.

Wu, John C.H., translator. Lao Tzu. *Tao Teh Ching*. Boston: Shambhala, 1989.

Bibliography

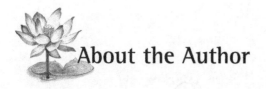

About the Author

Vimala McClure lives and writes in Boulder, Colorado. She is the author of the classic *Infant Massage: A Handbook for Loving Parents* and founder of the International Association of Infant Massage Instructors. She has been practicing and teaching Tantra yoga since 1971.

She has also written *A Woman's Guide to Tantra Yoga, The Ethics of Love: Using Yoga's Timeless Wisdom to Heal Yourself, Your Family & the Earth, Fabric Dyeing for Beginners,* and a book for children: *Bangladesh: Rivers in a Crowded Land.*

As well as being a writer, Vimala is a textile artist. Her quilts have won awards in regional and national shows, have been featured in national magazines, and are exhibited in galleries and private collections.

Vimala has two adult children and three grandchildren.